Tracy,

Thank you so much for you support.

Enjoy

Single Moms Survival Guide

Moving on with Life After Divorce

AYESHA GOODALL

www.goodzenconsulting.com

Table of Contents

Acknowledgments

I would like to first give thanks to my Heavenly Father Jehovah God. If it weren't for me trusting and leaning on him, I wouldn't be in any position to write a book to empower other women. I would like to thank my beautiful mother for teaching me survival and strength. Because of her strength, I am able to be strong. I would like to thank my dear friend, Deborah Franklin, for standing by my side during one of the most toughest and roughest times of my life. I am forever grateful for her love and support. My dear Dolly Booker, words can't describe what this woman has done for me and my children, she is my ROCK. Thank you. I would like to give a big warm thank you to my in-laws, Benny and Angela Mclemore for stepping up and taking care of my babies when I couldn't, for loving them unconditionally, and for your continued support as amazing grandparents. I would like to give a huge thank you to my spiritual army of soldiers that surrounded me when I was down and continued to encourage me to not give up and continue to push through. Thanks to my mental health team at Kaiser Permanente WLA for helping me to become aware of the fact that I was normal, that it's okay to not be okay at times, how to manage my emotions, and that what people think of me is none of my business. I have to thank my cousins Danielle Carr and Candice Williams, and my aunt, Tashi Carr, for being by my side in the grueling hours of fighting through the court system, and for loving my little ones unconditionally. My cousin, Robbie McCullough, for taking me and my children in during our transition. My Uncle and Aunt, Charles and Terry Vines, for supporting me when my dad was murdered and shaking me up to realize that only I am responsible for my decisions, that life events will happen, but it's all about how I respond, and for teaching me the E+R=O (event +response=outcome) method to life, as well as your continued support with the children. Pamela Threats for genuinely being my friend embracing us as if we were born from the same mother and father, now forever my sister. I must give a great big thanks to my business and life mentors, Rodney Foster, Lanier Carter Price, Mr. and Mrs. Edwin and Andrea Haynes, mere strangers in the beginning of my healing process who saw greatness in me, believed in me and helped me grow beyond measure in my journey to success. Troy Wilkinson, my financial and business mentor, thank you for all you have done and continue to do, and for over 20 years of friendship. Last, but definitely not least, thank you to Elam B. King and Adrienne E Bell for helping me level up and tell my story in an impactful way. Thank you for stepping in and sacrificing your time to help make my dream come true.

Dedication

I would like to dedicate this book to the single mothers who have preceded me that paved the way for us today to the best of their ability without being provided the type of resources that we are provided with today.

To all single mothers who are currently in transition from a divorce, the death of their spouse, or who are experiencing some type of loss and just do not have the direction or tools to turn their current darkness into light.

To all the young ladies who are growing up, let this book be a preventative tool to avoid the headache and nightmare of making premature, emotional decisions in choosing a mate and having children. This is a tool to teach you to be grounded when making this kind of life-changing decision.

Lastly, to all the mothers still in a marriage who feel lost or have lost a sense of self, need to re-center and re-discover their happy place.

The Impact of the Butterfly

The butterfly is a symbol of metamorphosis and transformation.
The symbol of new life, letting go of old cycles and finding your true inner expression.
The butterfly calls you to expand your awareness, spread your wings and call forth your inner joy.
Let go of limitations, and free yourself to express your own beauty within.
It is the time of spiritual transitions. Symbolic of moving from one phase of life to the next reaching higher, reaching outward, leaving the safety of the cocoon and finding your own place among the flowers of life.
Allowing the wind to carry you forward to your goals and dreams.
A time of self-discovery rebirth. The butterfly shows you the beauty within.

Foreward

I was so excited when Ayesha asked me to write this forward. I've had the pleasure of knowing Ayesha Goodall for 7 plus years. We met during a time when I was in the middle of some difficult circumstances. I was close to losing my home and my marriage. Fortunately, because of the journey she had already been through and the wisdom she gained, she was able to transfer some nuggets over to me to keep me encouraged. I was able to borrow her belief and apply her wisdom to inspire me to push pass those temporary circumstances. Ayesha is one of the few people that not only shared the importance of believing in yourself but also showed how to apply that belief to push through her life experiences.

And now she has transferred some of those same nuggets to the world through this book. This book shares how a single mother of 3 small children can persevere through not only being the daughter of a father that was murdered but also pushing pass a divorce and a multitude of other challenges along her journey. The level of resiliency and positive outlook that she has kept through it all has been amazing. I am still in awe of how she has turned some of her tragedies into triumphs.

If you didn't know, I'm here to share with you that it is not easy to be a single mom of 1 let alone 3 children. Of course, I have not personally been through it, but I've had the opportunity to be on the other side when I was dating my wife. When I met my wife 18 years ago, she had 2 small children ages 4 and 5. The children's father was not in their lives. I saw first-hand some of the struggles that my wife had to deal with in not only our dating but with life in general. Although she ultimately overcame those struggles, I believe that if she had a guide like this book it would have allowed her to avoid some pitfalls and challenges that she went through individually and for us as a dating couple. Whether the subject is child rearing, dating, finances, friendships, work-life balance, personal development, or helping to keep yourself in a positive mental state and not become overwhelmed, this book will provide you ways to maximize your role as a single mom. Ayesha takes you on her journey as a single mom using not only humor but stone-cold facts of her hardships she experienced. She shows you how to not break down but break through your existing circumstances and come out a winner. Her last name is Goodall, and I believe this book is Good for All single moms and even offers some good tips for ALL MOMS. I am so happy and grateful to know Ayesha Goodall and I pray you are blessed by the words she shares in The Single Moms Survival Guide.

Read this book, and go be great!

Elam B. King
Relationship Coach, Motivational Speaker
Author of Understanding a Man: Empowering Women with Tools for Lasting Relationships
www.understandingaman.com

INTRODUCTION

Are you a single mom? Have you recently gone through, or are you currently going through a divorce?

This is a book of valuable resources for the single mom. The only thing worse than a divorce is death. As a single mom of three, I wrote this book to help the single mom not only survive, but thrive, reconnect with her children, and move on with life after divorce. Life is filled with problems; this book is filled with solutions.

I am not a psychologist, nor a doctor, but I am a single mom, and I have gone through what you are currently going through. I have stood in your shoes and felt your pain. I have dealt with all the feelings of loneliness, hopelessness, despair, pain, sorrow, misery, resentment, blame, and guilt a divorce can throw at you. I am here to tell you that not only can you survive but you are also able to thrive! You have the ability to rebound successfully with the resources and tips I share in this book. You will also get a good dose of my personal experience. I've heard the stories from many women like yourself. Phenomenal women who were totally blindsided by divorce.

The purpose of this book is not to go into the statistics of how divorce negatively affects future generations. There are tons of books and studies that showcase these awful statistics, but that is not my purpose.

Instead, this book is a roadmap and a toolkit for your very survival. If I can get through it, so can you. This is your blueprint to succeed as a single parent.

I am not a financial advisor, so when I talk about finances or give examples and make suggestions on things you can do to create more cash and relieve stress, it's purely anecdotal. Please check with a qualified, licensed professional when making money and life decisions that affect you and your children.

"We Are an Army "

According to the US Census Bureau, 53 percent of marriages end in divorce in America. There are approximately 12 million single-parent households in the United States, alone, more than 80 percent of which are single mother households, which means over 17 million children are raised by single mothers. Ladies, we are an army! PLEASE KNOW THAT YOU ARE NOT ALONE. The majority of us find ourselves raising our children with little to no support from dad or any other family members.

On a global scale, here are the ratios of single mother homes by culture, according to Don Lemon's commentary found on politifact.com: Asian American/Pacific Islanders make up 17 percent, Non-Hispanics/Whites make up 29 percent, Hispanics make up 53 percent, Native Indian and Native Alaskans makeup 66 percent, and African-Americans make up 73 percent. This is just scratching the surface. The numbers are climbing. I am not even going into the statistics of how many of these single mothers are homeless, living in shelters, and on welfare. There are a large number of single mothers who have just given up and lost the hope of creating a bright future for themselves and their children. This is why I am passionate to share that there is a way to create light out of such a dark space. Despite society's distorted view of single motherhood, there are a lot of single mothers turning their breakdowns into breakthroughs, and I AM one of them. From a positive perspective, here is what I affirm not only for me but all single mothers:

- **All I need is within me.**
- **I AM stronger than I seem.**
- **I AM braver than I think.**
- **I have unshakable faith.**
- **Miracles are taking place.**
- **I AM done complaining.**
- **I AM grateful.**
- **I appreciate my life.**

Notes

Notes

CHAPTER 1

"Perfectly Imperfect-In the Beginning"

I was raised in Los Angeles, California by a single mother. At the age of five, my mother married my stepfather. I was raised in a very dysfunctional household. My stepfather was what you'd call a functioning alcoholic and was abusive to my mother. Don't get it twisted, though; my mother was not a punk, and she held her ground. My biological father ran the streets of L.A. as a gang member and drug dealer by choice. He did not want to marry my mother. My mother had my brother by my stepdad when I was seven years old. My mom worked a job, took care of the home, and ran her side business as a licensed manicurist. My stepfather worked a job as well and, from what I could surmise as a child, handled the majority of the monetary needs of the household. Even though we are seven years apart, my brother and I grew up very close.

Although my biological father chose the streets and was in and out of jail, I remember my mom would do her best to allow me to see him when he would come around. Regardless of his lifestyle, I loved my dad. He made me feel like I would always be his little princess.

The memories I have of my stepfather are not all good. I remember how he would hang out until the wee hours of the night, come in the house stammering and holding the walls because he was drunk out of his mind, and I would hear him go to the bathroom and vomit. It made me so nervous. The majority of my teenage years, all my parents did was argue and fight. I had little to no respect for my stepfather because of what I saw him put my mother through. Although my mother was a strong woman, I could just see and feel the toll of what his erratic behavior did to her. As the oldest of two children, my mom would project her stress on me the majority of the time. I suffered emotionally, causing me to become introverted and creating a lot of resentment towards my mother. I can say now; my mom did the best she could with what she was taught.

One Saturday when I was sixteen years old, my stepfather and mother were having a really bad argument, which turned into a really bad physical altercation. My mom was so stressed out behind it she was in tears. After some hours had passed, my stepfather pulled me to the side to talk to me to let me know he wanted to adopt me and for me to change my last name to his last name. I felt it was a huge disrespect to my living biological father, and I did not respect my stepfather enough to agree to that. When I told him I did not want to and why he became angry and pinned me up to the wall, telling me I was disrespectful. I kicked and fought him off of me. I then went to my mother, who was still incredibly upset about the earlier altercation. I asked her why she continued to stay with him and even subject my brother and I to this abusive behavior. She stated she did not know how to leave and that she wanted to wait until my little brother was out of high school. I told her she needed to find a way.

Shortly after that conversation, my mother put my brother and me into Alanon and Alateen programs as she went to a co-dependency program, with high hopes for us to heal. It worked for a moment and went right back through the vicious cycle of abuse. When I graduated from high school, I was adamant about staying away from home and would spend many nights at my friend's house. When I turned 18, I met a guy. My first sex partner. Once my mother's intuition kicked in and realized I lost my virginity, she was enraged.

I went out with my friends a few nights a week after she learned I had lost my virginity, and, when I came home at midnight one night, all of my belongings were on the front porch, and she asked me to leave. I never returned home. I began my journey to find Ayesha and search for true happiness.

My mother remained in that toxic relationship until my brother was thirteen. I was twenty at the time and no longer living in the house. One evening, I made a visit to the house to have dinner. My mother made me aware that she and my stepfather had been separated and had recently lost the house we grew up in to foreclosure. My mother then became a singlemother as a result of a divorce.

Notes

Notes

CHAPTER 2

"I Didn't Marry to Divorce"

I was raised in a very strict religious environment. When dating, we had to date with the view to get married. There was absolutely no casual dating allowed, and you would be shunned if you committed fornication. Although I made a few mistakes in the area of sex before marriage, I recovered and practiced celibacy for years. My dream was to meet the man of my dreams, have two kids, and grow old together.

When I met my husband, Jerome, we were 19 and 20. We dated for about a year. We shared the same religious beliefs and met at one of the youth social gatherings. He had a way about him I could not turn down. I had been living on my own for almost two years; he still lived with his mother and father. All I know was this man was FINE. He stood about 6'3", 200 pounds, with nice, even-toned, caramel-color skin, light brown eyes, and a bald head. Yumminess. I'm 5'3", so I loved the idea of a tall, dark and handsome man embracing me. I felt a sense of protection from him. He was also like a big teddy bear, soft and cuddly. For me, looks were everything at that age. Can we say a little shallow? Needless to say, after a year-and-a-half we parted ways because I felt I was too young to settle down and get married—I wanted to have fun and live life; whereas, he wanted to get married.

Years passed, and I ventured off into life and was involved in other relationships. It seemed like every two years, Jerome and I would cross paths in social settings. Because we did not part on bad terms, we had always been friendly with each other, sometimes flirty. The last we saw each other, I was 27 years old, which was when I entered into a seriously committed relationship with my eldest daughter's dad. Five years had gone by, and I was working out at the local gym in Pasadena. As I walked down the stairs to exit the gym, low and behold, I see Jerome. When we noticed each other, it was a feeling of bliss, like we ignited a flame that never went away. Even though that was the feeling, we just said hello to each other and moved on. Time moved on, and my best friend Debra told me she had started seriously dating a firefighter out of the Compton Fire Department. Jerome was a probationary firefighter out of the same fire department. Six months later,

Debra announced she and her boyfriend were getting married and that she wanted me to be her Maid of Honor. She disclosed that Jerome was the best man. Oh boy. Although I still had feelings for him, I believed he was my past, and I really wasn't keen on revisiting the past after almost fifteen years. As we prepared for the wedding, Jerome and I were able to get reacquainted and started to casually date. We dated about eight months and then he proposed to me over a romantic dinner in November 2006.

This all sounds so perfectly packaged, but it wasn't. Knowing what I know today, I had grown and evolved mentally, emotionally, and financially. I had just sold my house and ended a relationship around the time we decided to date. He had been dating, as well, but at the age of 33, he still lived with his parents and was just rehired as a "probationary" firefighter and EMT. Nothing too much had changed for him, from when we were nineteen. I ignored the fact that he hadn't really had any sense of responsibility as a grown man. I ignored that sign amongst others. This is not to speak poorly about who he is as a person, but to impress upon you that I did not pay attention to those type of details. I chose to pay attention to what his exterior looked like and how he made me feel at that moment a very shallow way of thinking in which I made the agreement with myself of loving this man. I had some reservations. I told him during our courtship that no matter how hard it got, I would never want to entertain moving back home with mama as a grown married couple raising a family. He reassured me that would not happen.

Fast forward to a month before our wedding: I got laid off from my job, and Jerome had to take on the load of most of the bills. This is where the test began in the relationship because we still had a wedding to pay for. We worked it out and were able to move forward with the wedding. May 7, 2007, I became "Mrs. Wife". Jerome moved into my place because I was taking care of my elderly grandmother who lived with me. Almost two months after we were married, I became pregnant with our first child together, Suraya. After we learned we were pregnant my grandmother decided she wanted to get her own apartment in a senior community. Once she moved out, the income I received to care for her ended.

My husband told me he wanted us to move near his mom in Altadena, California, but, in order for us to save for the house he wanted to get, we would have to move in with his parents for three months. He reminded me that he remembered that I did not want to move back home but because I wanted to practice submissiveness I obliged after he convinced me that I would be able to receive more help with the baby from his mother.

We moved in with his parents in December of 2007. I was really not at peace about it but made it work the best I could. Mind you; I was six months pregnant. My in-laws are amazing supporters, especially when it comes to their son. However, the saying that two queens cannot live under one roof holds true, in my opinion. The three months turned into ten months of living with his parents, which took a toll on all of us.

The house Jerome was waiting to be available for us a lease-to-own, had some issues. I gave birth to Suraya in March 2008, and we moved into the home in May 2008. The house had to be painted and carpeted, and I was a new mother. My husband at the time told the landlords they did not have to paint or carpet, that we would do it. So, I was literally barefoot with a newborn, painting and helping polish hardwood floors. My husband was working two jobs, and we were really doing our best to make ends meet (reality check, ENDS DON'T MEET). Our marriage continued to undergo many tests. I told my husband it wasn't realistic for us to be able to maintain the cost of the rent on that home and take care of a family, and that I thought it was best to downsize. Because I was very afraid of not knowing where we were going to live—we weren't going back to his mother's house—I suggested to my husband that we move to L.A. and get a more affordable place than we had in Altadena. He felt more comfortable living close to his mother but opted to agree with me.

I was ready to get out of the city of Altadena as quickly as possible. I reached out to a family friend who owned several properties and we found an amazing duplex unit in Leimert Park (a beautiful city within Los Angeles County). This is where I know and hold true that our marriage became compromised. I noticed that once we moved and got settled in our new place, my husband's behavior began to change. We started having our weekly family Bible study, and, after a couple of months of being settled in our new place, he stopped it. I then went back to work after being off on maternity leave. He started to work more and travel more with a side gig. He became more emotionally distant.

He lost focus on his career as a fireman as well as our family once he became an assistant road manager. Due to his negligence on the job he got fired and started to collect unemployment. As we know men are not whole if they feel that they cannot provide for their family. I started to see resentment and frustration develop with him because of the way he spoke to me and at times, he wouldn't speak to me at all. He stopped going to worship with us as a family on Wednesdays and Sundays. I then began to feel like a single mom in my marriage. My husband became verbally abusive, which led to minor physical abuse even in front of our children. So much so that I had to call the police to our home on at least two occasions. We are talking about a 6 foot 2 200lb man and a 5 foot 3, 120 lb. woman with my little ones in the home. I suffered from so much stress and frustration that I developed high blood pressure.

One evening, he and I were arguing about him coming home in the wee hours of the night. Our kids were in the room at the time when the argument escalated and he pinned me against the wall. I lashed out and scratched him in the face. He immediately backed off and called the police to have me arrested for assault. He specifically told me I would go to jail because firefighters and policemen operate under a specific code and if anyone was going to jail it would be me. The police arrive, he goes in on what I have done, and I tell my side of the story. The police then instruct our children that are 6 and 7 years old (my daughter from previous relationship and his son from a previous relationship) to tell them what they saw. After the police get their story, they decided to arrest my husband for putting his hands on me. My husband spent 72 hours in jail.

After his time in jail, he comes back, and we talk about our future moving forward. He expresses his feelings, and I discuss mine, so he and I both agreed to work towards a healthy marriage. We decided to take the necessary steps to grow past our challenges. We decided to pursue Spiritual Counseling within our church and professional marriage counseling. Because we agreed that we loved each other and didn't get married to get divorced, the help we received seemed to be working. We also decided we did not want any more children and began searching for the best birth control. He had even considered a vasectomy, but by thetime we made the final decision as to which method we would use, we received the news that we were pregnant again. As we moved forward, my husband's behavior had relapsed into being disengaged. He began to be out of town more, coming home really late, not present emotionally, spiritually nor physically. Bills started to go behind. One day he came home, and he stated that he no longer wanted to be a part of the family. He felt overwhelmed with the problems, and he wasn't ready to take on having another child, and all that comes with that, so he left. Just like that. I was devastated and very hurt. I fought what seemed to be a never ending battle of whether or not I could move forward with three children, work, and run an entire household alone successfully. I also battled mentally about whether or not I would keep the baby for so many reasons. What stood out the most was that I had built such a solid foundation with God, how could I get rid of his creation? To be transparent, I made an appointment at the clinic, but my conscience did not allow me to go through with the procedure. I put my big girl pants on and decided to just accept the fact that **I GOT THIS!**

Notes

CHAPTER 3

"Lost in the Sauce-The Emotional Adjustment"

Feeling afraid, alone, abandoned and judged by some of my friends and family, I continued to push through or pretended to push through. I really had no choice, I still had two other children to feed as well as tending to my health as I had a growing baby inside of me. I spoke to my landlord, who had known me from my school-aged years, she knew my work ethic, so I let her know what had been taking place. She told me to pay her as I can. Although she expressed that, I did not want to fail her from the business aspect, so I did what I could do under the circumstances. I continued to go to work as normal until I could not bear the stress of work and home, I took an early maternity leave. I became numb and continued to prepare myself for my new life. I found myself in denial thinking my husband would come to his senses and come back. I did not want my children to be raised in a single parent home. I prayed for peace, for soundness of mind and for discernment. One day while I was home on maternity leave, I logged on to the internet. We had access to one another's email accounts, and I found a stream of emails from a young lady who was a mutual friend of ours. This young lady was also a member of our religious organization, and we all hung out together from time to time. The emails were extremely graphic about their intimate relations and how they looked forward to being together and seeing each other again. I also started receiving messages from an anonymous woman on Social Media so much so that because I did not reply she would harass me about needing to have words with me. She reached out to mutual friends and business partners to try to reach me, to the point that I had to have the Social Media provider to completely remove her from trying to contact me. Mind you, the moment I started praying for discernment and peace these signs started coming up. I was six months pregnant at this time, and I was still doing my best to hold it together. I started to think that he may have another family hoping that he didn't pass any sexually transmitted diseases to me. I felt betrayed. I cried and cried and prayed and prayed to get past it, keeping in mind that the health of my unborn child was important.

A friend within my congregation whom I knew I could trust with this process, stood by my side during these moments. Internally I still didn't feel like I was enough. Because of my intuition and thoughts of him possibly having another family, I found another message from an anonymous person on Social Media stating the possibility of my husband getting another woman pregnant. I didn't want to accept that but the hard reality of that being the case was not far fetched. I was eight months pregnant when I found this out. Due to my core beliefs and the principles that we practiced, I had to have hardcore evidence that my husband had extramarital affairs for us to have a scriptural divorce. I filed for legal separation at the time. I showed my ministers within the congregation all the emails and social media messages, but they told me that wasn't enough evidence. They tried to reach out to my then husband but he dodged their calls.

On May 19, 2010, my son Jayden was born. My mother-in-law was there to support me along with my spiritual sister Dolly. I scheduled a tubal ligation right after delivery. Immediately after surgery, I was taken to recovery. Early the next morning, I was moved to a regular room. Due to the intensity of the delivery and immediately into surgery, I experienced a lot of bleeding and was advised that I could not be under any type of stress as I healed. My mother-in-law and Dolly took turns caring for me and my baby. As the morning progressed, my then husband came to visit me. He told me that he did not believe the child was his and that he would do everything in his power to not work a real job so he would not have to help support me with the children. At that moment I became stressed and emotional. The nurse and Dolly had to ask him to leave.

Two days later, Jayden and I were discharged. My friend Deborah came over to assist me. My oldest daughter was 8, and youngest daughter was 2. After Jayden turned three months, we had to move out of the duplex we had lived in because I didn't want to accrue any more late fees, nor lose my integrity with the landlord. Fortunately, I found a smaller place in Inglewood from a referral source. In the midst of us getting settled and me having to go back to work once Jayden became five months, I was in a very emotional, vulnerable state. I allowed Jerome to come back into my life and pretend to help, but he only toyed with my emotions. I let that go on for about a month too long and I finally stopped it. As time passed on many people would make me aware of seeing Jerome out with multiple women even some that knew who I was (We were still technically married, and I had false hope of us still getting back together). I removed myself from the people who were telling me these things because it just kept me in a state of feeling lost and depressed. I victimized myself instead of rising above the situation and thinking soundly. Little did I know I was undergoing a serious case of postpartum depression. I didn't know what it was because I did not really experience it after my other pregnancies. I had a conversation with my mother-in-law stating that I strongly believed he had another baby outside of the marriage. She stated she strongly doubted it because he can't keep a secret like that from her. I left it alone.

At this point, Jayden is 5 ½ months, and I received an email while at work from an uncle on my father's side stating he had been trying to contact me for weeks. In the body of the email, he states that my father has been murdered and that they needed me to identify the body and sign off on some paperwork because I was the eldest child living. His stepdaughter lied to the Coroner and said she was authorized to sign off on the paperwork, in reality, she was not a biological child. I had to carry on the responsibility of traveling to Bakersfield, CA to plan a funeral in the midst of all the personal drama with the marriage. I put on my big girl pants once again and handled the business of my father's murder the best way I knew how. When I asked my then husband and in-laws to help me with the children, they refused to make themselves available. I had to travel back and forth with small children to Bakersfield which is about a two- hour drive away. I did have two of my younger cousins on my maternal side help me through the first couple of trips.

One breakdown after another was taking place. I was able to get food aide at the time because I needed the assistance. I was able to take a few days off of work. My performance at work was definitely affected. I had multiple write-ups for oversight and tardiness. My supervisor was not the easiest to get along with. I started resenting her. My emotions were spiraling downward. I started feeling out of control and all over the place. I allowed emotions to get the best of me. I truly got "lost in the sauce."

One afternoon after I left work to pick up the children, I made a phone call to the Kaiser mental health line. At the time I was working at Kaiser Hospital. I felt like I needed to get my mind right. I felt overwhelmed with the children and overwhelmed at work. I felt like doing some serious harm to my husband so he could feel my pain. At this time Jayden was seven months old, my youngest girl was 2 ½ years old, and my oldest was 8 ½ years old. I'd communicated these feelings to the person on the hotline service and told them I just needed to schedule something sooner than three weeks, which was when my next appointment was scheduled. Something I said during the call prompted them to advise me to come to the ER for an evaluation. I was compliant because I really needed the help.

I called Dolly, my spiritual sister and explained to her what I needed to do. Without hesitation, she took the kids, dropped me off at the ER and headed home. She told me to call her once I was done. I went to the ER and checked in. They immediately called me to the back and checked me into an evaluation room where the Doctor and Nurse were ready and waiting. I was perplexed and clueless as to why I was seen so quickly. The psychologist who came in to perform the evaluation was very pleasant. He stated that I was very overwhelmed and needed a short break away from my day to day routine. I agreed. He asked if I had somewhere for the kids to comfortably stay, I said yes. He then proceeded to tell me that they had a place for me to go where I would be able to decompress for a couple of days. Still clueless I told them I had a ride and to just provide the address. He said, "No" and that I had to ride in an ambulance. I was really thrown off at this point. After the Psychologist left, the nurse came from behind the station with the phone stating that my sister with my children wanted to speak to me. I then took the phone, and she stated that the ERT (Emergency Response Team) was at her house wanting to take the children. I didn't know who the ERT was and why they wanted to take my children. Dolly stated that she had a relative who worked with children services and that she was familiar with what was taking place. She told me she was going to strongly suggest they consider keeping the children together with a blood relative they were familiar with and not to put them in a strange foster home. My oldest daughter's dad took her, and because my husband refused to step up, my in-laws volunteered to take the two little ones. Even though my in-laws had my 2yr old and my 7-month-old, they were still reported in the foster care system because they were not under the care of a biological parent.

There was a gentleman who got on the phone who was a part of the ERT, who was very high strung and adamant about my diagnosis. I understood that before the decision was to be made to take my children, he was ordered to come and evaluate me. Well, he never showed up. I was taken to the mental health facility as a compliant 51/50 patient. What that means is, I cooperated with the doctors but they still considered me "CRAZY". OMG! What just happened? This was an interesting transition. After they had me stripped of practically everything, this same gentleman that was a part of the ERT finally came to see me once I was in the "Crazy House". He interrogated me and was extremely chauvinistic. He said, "I know by the way you look you are trouble. I'm sure you give your husband a hard time. Now tell me what happened." I felt like whatever the diagnosis was, he did his best to force a negative reaction from me, but I refused. The very high strung gentleman finally left, and I was assigned a room along with a roommate. Suddenly I became very sad and extremely afraid. I did not know why all this had taken place.

After a few hours had passed, I called my mother, she was of no emotional support because she did not understand why I would let things get to this point. I called my aunt who told me to call her once they told me the diagnosis and how long I was scheduled to be there. I met a very kind Psychiatrist who discovered I did not belong there. The notes on my initial evaluation did not match up with the behavior she witnessed from me. She stated that I suffered from an adjustment disorder which is common with what I had experienced. The ERT and ER had it recorded that I suffered from suicidal ideation. I guess when I said I wanted to harm my husband that was the trigger but that was still the wrong diagnosis.

I was discharged after 36 hours and was assigned an outpatient day retreat for six weeks. It was for the therapy I originally wanted but a little more intensive. I learned a lot in the program down to how they determine doses of medication they give to mental health patients. Pretty much they disclosed that they use the patients as test rats to determine how much of a dosage to give based on the patient's reaction. Fortunately, I was told I did not need medication. A sleeping pill was recommended, but I didn't need that either.

At the end of my program, my specialist pulled me into his office for a private meeting and asked for my permission to be frank. I said, "Yes." He told me that I am capable to accomplish anything I put my mind to. He said that I need to stop giving a damn (he used more of a harsh word) about what others think, no matter who it was. He told me I needed to forgive myself and forgive those that I feel have hurt me. He encouraged me to have a talk with them and share how I truly felt in a respectful way. He also told me to let them know I forgive them and that I release the negative feelings I had toward them so that I could heal, grow and be healthy for my children. One of the people he told me to address first outside of myself was my mother, then my husband. What a challenge. I thanked him immensely. I then had to start the process of fighting to get my kids back. It took about 3 months for me to address my mother and about 5 months to address my then husband. It wasn't easy, but when I did I felt a weight lifted.

As I was in and out of court proving my worth to the courts to get my kids back, I learned that it would take approximately 18 months to get my children back. I did not let that hold me back. My mom showed me that she would not support me in this process at all which made it easy for me to release her temporarily so I could gain the strength from God and outside sources that truly supported me. I was introduced to a community of positive, forward thinking individuals who taught me about believing in myself again. These individuals taught me the value of mentorship and personal development. Mind you these were total strangers that are now forever family to me. I was compliant on all levels with the courts because I was determined not to wait 18 months to get my children back. I complied with everything the courts ordered me to do. From parenting classes to anger management classes and even domestic violence classes. My then husband was not compliant on ANY level. My social worker told me she would do what she could to shorten the time away from my kids. I had supervised visitation at first and then one overnight visit with the kids. It was grueling yet very humbling. With favor and grace, I got my kids back within six months instead of waiting that full 18 months. October 2011 my kids came back home permanently. I still had to have periodic visits after that, but that didn't interfere with me conquering this huge challenge life presented me in getting my children back. My case closed fully Jan 2012. I proceeded to get the divorce, and my husband was served yet non-responsive. I was awarded the divorce with full custody of the children.

The moral of this chapter is, no matter how hard it gets in the midst of your divorce, don't let your emotions override you so much that you lose sight of what's in the best interest of your children. Lean heavily on your higher power; mine is GOD. Find a support team you trust to help you through this difficult time.

Notes

Notes

CHAPTER 4

<u>"Mommy Money Matters"</u>

"Marriage is grand, divorce about a hundred grand."

Few things can drain the bank, like a divorce. Depending on which divorce/marriage expert or financial guru you talk to, you hear things like A divorce will set you back seven years, etc. Like your boat capsizing in the middle of the Pacific Ocean, a divorce can leave you feeling helpless, vulnerable, and susceptible to economic attack. Assuming finances have been a challenge for you, statistically, most divorces happen as a result of financial crisis. This section will help you take an honest inventory of where you are and how to improve your financial situation. The first step you need to take to steady your finances as a divorcing single mom is:

1. **Conduct an inventory and Create a budget**

On one side of a sheet of paper, write down all of the income and sources of revenue you have coming in each month, and, on the other side, write down every expense you can predict over the next 90, 180, and 365 days.

Once you're done, add 20 percent to the expenses, because there will be unexpected and unplanned surprises. From attorney fees to hiring babysitters, to moving fees, to additional work-related expenses, to going back to school to improve your hire ability and résumé, it is important to budget for the unforeseeable but almost certain, extra expenses. Now, if you are fortunate enough to be in the black, good for you! Most newly divorced moms find themselves on the negative side of the balance sheet with this exercise.

"If your outgoing expenses exceeds your income - your upkeep will be your downfall."
Tony Cooke

I recently heard on the radio that the average household debt in the

U.S. not including mortgage-related debt has increased 20 percent a year. Families are spending more, but they are spending it on credit cards. While these numbers are good news for retailers in the short-term, the long-term financial impact for our families, our futures, and our nation is dismal. It is important to keep a close eye on finances throughout your divorce, or you may find yourself swimming in debt.

2. Downsize your overhead where you can

This means eliminating all unnecessary and extra expenses, to survive financially. Talk with a good attorney and tax strategist or financial ad¬visor to find out where it makes sense to cut expenses. Are you leasing a car? Perhaps, you are able to downgrade your car and drive an older model that is paid for, so you don't have a car payment for a few years. It could mean selling the house or leasing it out, in exchange for something smaller that does not require you to pour your money down an endless money pit and spend hours each month on maintenance. Remember, your kids will grow up and be gone before you know it. You can always reinvest in a big house or estate at a future date. Are you living on credit cards? Are you using credit cards to pay for groceries or utilities? Are you making only the minimum payments on credit cards? If yes, you are headed toward financial trouble, fast.

3. Become the Cash Queen– Stop Living on Credit

We live in a -buy now, pay later, I-want-it-all-now society. Few people have the discipline or patience to wait and pay for something only when they can afford it. But, believe it or not, that is the good old-fashioned way to getting rich.
If you can't afford it, don't buy it. Live a disciplined life, and don't spend money you really don't have. Credit cards are not cash; they are debts. They are shackles, a ball, and chain that will keep you down. And, if you can't pay them off each month, they will slowly choke the financial air out of you, like a hungry python. When I say become the "Cash Queen" that means pay cash for everything. Don't go in debt for anything, un-less it is an income-producing vehicle, like a rental property or other invest¬ment. Pay the credit cards off each month, so you don't rack up interest payments. Make the decision that the first month you can't pay the creditcards off, you will cut them up. Few have the discipline to do

this, but, if you do, you are someone who can actually feel good about earning airline miles and other perks from credit card companies. DaveRamsey.com is a valuable resource. His Financial Peace University has helped millions out of debt fast along with his helpful site EveryDollar.com.

4. Get an extra job to earn some extra cash

Moonlighting also called working a second job is a great way for a cash strapped mom or a mom who wants to build a financial reserve to hedge against future financial crisis to get ahead. Not only can a part-time job provide extra income, it can become an outlet both socially and mentally to get a break from staring at the four walls of an empty, quiet, lonely apartment. I've done many odd jobs and extra projects to earn money for myself and my family throughout the years, in addition to my regular career.

5. Adjust your W-2 withholdings

If you are working a job and are a W-2 employee, you can increase your withholding allowances to put more money on your paycheck. I never wanted to give the government an interest-free loan. Some people like to get a few thousand back when they file their income tax return not me; I always wanted my cash now. Ask an expert, but this can be a great way to increase cash flow. DISCLAIMER: I am not an attorney, a financial advisor, nor a CPA. You should check with qualified and competent advisors on all financial matters. If you have kids, there will be emergencies, so please plan accordingly.

6. Sell your junk

That's right, have a good old-fashioned garage sale. You would be surprised how much you can make by selling your junk. Many friends I suggest this to end up cashing in hundreds, even thousands of dollars, just by eliminating their junk.

7. Debt consolidation loan

You can eliminate high-interest credit cards by obtaining a debt consolidation loan. This is good for managing high-interest-rate credit cards and only having one payment, instead of 16. The challenge with this is that many people will increase their spending and recharge their credit cards, landing them in more debt than before. If you can avoid making this mistake, it is a good option for you.

8. Emergency fund

Have an emergency savings fund for accidents, incidents, and emergencies.

Become spend-thrift and budget wisely. My ultimate goal is to have my money work for me and to teach my children the language of money; how to multiply, compound and ivest their money wisely.

Notes

Notes

CHAPTER 5

"Overcoming Anger and Facing Your Fear"

Nothing paralyzes more than fear, and nothing is more freeing than facing your fear and overcoming it. Fear of the unknown is what jolted me the most after my divorce.

As mentioned before, I questioned myself as to whether or not I was an adequate mother. I was always curious if I was a capable wife or if I'd ever love a man again. I wondered if I'd ever get married again and what people truly thought of me. I also had to come to grips with the fact that I became extremely bitter and angry. I never considered myself to be an angry person. But because of the resentment that was built towards my ex-husband, it caused me to become angry.

Dealing with the fear factor kept me in a low frequency state. I said to myself, "I must overcome this fear!" When it comes to overcoming fear, many times the real issue is control. As a strong woman, mother, caretaker and business woman also known as the "Alpha Female" we feel like we need some type of control over matters of the home. Divorce then throws us for a loop, a downward spiral that makes us feel out of control. There are many things that happen when we feel out of control:

- **We isolate ourselves**
- **We become emotionally overwhelmed**
- **We are inefficient in our work performance**
- **We slack in caring for the children**
- **We become absent minded**
- **We become dependent on alcohol or drugs**
- **We exercise poor judgment**
- **We may fall into depression**
- **We may have suicidal thoughts**

This is not an exhaustive list but these are a few things that can happen when we allow the fear of losing control to overwhelm us.

When you decide to face anxiety head on, you can minimize the paralyzing effects of fear.

Here are some tips you can use to help neutralize your fears and anxiety after divorce that has helped me:

1. Utilize deep breathing techniques to calm yourself

- I always wanted to take a yoga class to learn calming techniques. I learned that utilizing calming deep breaths and stretching are therapeutic. One simple breathing technique is inhaling fully, then holding it for about ten seconds, finally, slowly exhaling. Take 5- 10 deep breaths which allows oxygen to get into the brain and blood flow.

2. Talk to a licensed counselor, therapist or a spiritual counselor/ pastor

- By talking to a professional who is trained in divorce recovery, you can deal proactively with fear, anger and other self-sabotaging emotions. Going to a counselor or therapist is not an admission to guilt, it is a sign of strength and wisdom on your part. Don't suffer in silence; please reach out for help.
- Self-maintenance is essential. Just like you have to do periodic maintenance on your car for it to perform optimally and avoid breakdowns, the same applies to us.

3. Recognize the spiritual dimension of your life.

- Don't lose sight of your spiritual relationship with God or whomever your Higher Power is.
- By getting in touch and staying in touch with our spiritual needs, we allow deep work to activate within us that is not merely surface or cosmetic. After all, the heart transformation can and will make a difference as we live our best lives and pursue purpose.

Notes

Notes

<u>"Forgiveness Leads to Freedom"</u>

As things moved forward on my journey, I still felt like I was emotionally imprisoned. I still felt a good amount of weight that needed to be lifted. I was still participating in my therapy sessions, and I had a pretty good recovery. Eventually, I expressed to my therapist that I felt like I was still carrying some weight. Please understand that I was doing my best to push through the pain. She asked me specifically if I felt I had fully forgiven my husband on the same level I'd forgiven my mother. During one of my sessions, we discovered I had some unresolved issues with my mother, but more importantly, I hadn't forgiven myself for feeling like I had failed my marriage. I realized that I blamed my ex-husband for leaving me and our kids. I also blamed my mother for feelings of not being loved by her like I wanted to be. I was angry with her for exposing my brother and me to unhealthy relationships under the false leadership of my dad and my stepdad.

As an American culture, we are obsessed with villains and heroes. I thought my husband, mother, and stepfather were the villains, and my dad was my hero despite all his flaws. While characters represent either good or evil which makes a compelling, watchable action story, I realize now that such broad categorizing of human behavior isn't healthy when you're working on moving on after divorce. For many, it is easier to believe that a villain, either outside or inside the marriage, is to blame for a divorce.

Dating back to Adam and Eve humans have found it necessary to make someone responsible when something goes wrong. Adam blamed Eve and Eve blamed the snake. To recover and flourish after divorce, the blame game must be exchanged for forgiveness.

Forgiveness is perhaps the most healing act you can bestow on yourself and your ex-partner as well as others. Unforgiveness breeds resentment. Holding onto resentment and anger is very destructive to our well

-being. It is a trigger to stress. As we know, stress leads to disease and is deadly. It's worth letting go of negative feelings and getting on with your life rather than holding on to emotions that can kill you.

Once I finally came to grips with forgiveness being a non-negotiable factor as I moved forward, I realized that I needed to conduct 4 Major "Cleansing" Tasks:

1. Have a conversation with God and ask Him to forgive me for anything I may have done that I was not aware of. I also had to come clean about the status of my heart and how I no longer wanted the pain, anger or bitterness.

2. Have a conversation with myself and truly forgive myself for what I contributed to the marriage failing.

3. Have another conversation full of love and forgiveness towards myself for losing my children temporarily.

4. Have a conversation with my mother, ex-husband, and step-father apologizing for allowing resentment to fester. I made a pact with myself to offer forgiveness for how I believed they've wronged me.

I was able to complete all tasks except for one. I was unable to speak to my stepfather because I could not locate him. Even though I forgave him in my heart, I am committed to fulfilling the task of writing him a letter.

- **Understand the difference between forgiving and condoning.**

Too often people feel if they forgive someone for their hurtful behavior, they are condoning what occurred. Condoning means accepting and overlooking while forgiving is an action that means you stop feeling anger or resentment which releases you from carrying the weight of the betrayal.

- **Accept that forgiveness creates internal harmony.**

When people get caught up in the idea that forgiveness means letting someone who harmed them off the hook for damaging behavior, turn the attention inward. Forgiveness is about making an active decision to let go of resentment because it is harmful to you.

- **Forgiveness doesn't mean you stop feeling hurt.**

Forgiveness is an action that is a part of the healing process. It does not mean you stop feeling sad. You may still cry or experience stages of grief from time to time. There is no expectation that you need to minimize your feelings.

- **Forgiveness does not equal trust.**

Appreciate that while you may actively forgive your former spouse for past behaviors, trust in the relationship has been broken. To forgive does not mean you must believe what your former spouse says, it just means that you are not going to carry resentment within you.

- **Maybe they truly don't know better.**

To err is human. To repeatedly show bad judgment and hurt others is indicative of a bigger issue. If your former spouse consistently shows self-absorbed, disrespectful, even lying behaviors, consider that they may lack the ability to do better. Even if they meet all the characteristics of a true villain, let go of blame by feeling thankful that you will no longer invest in a situation that will not change. If they do not have the capacity to change, forgive them for not having a moral compass or conscience to guide them.

I was determined to move on after my divorce. I was willing to tap into every resource I could possibly touch to help me to successfully move forward. If you want to move on after divorce and find happiness within yourself and a new relationship, start with forgiveness. It is the greatest gift you can give yourself. Forgiveness is also the gateway to mental and emotional freedom from the pains of divorce. I feel so much freedom now from all that emotional imprisonment I subjected myself to.

Notes

Notes

Notes

CHAPTER 7

"Stepping into Wholeness"

"Wholeness does not mean perfection: it means embracing the brokenness as an integral part of life." ~*Parker Palmer* This quote means everything to me. It brought me to the epitome of inner peace. Accepting myself first, flaws and all was the beginning of me stepping into my wholeness. I've discovered that spending ME time is essential for my personal growth and development. I have learned to appreciate getting to know Ayesha on multiple levels. I have embraced being confident enough to be able to look at myself in the mirror, and love ALL of who I AM. I have made a pact with myself to continue to fall in love with all of who I AM. I truly believe that what others think of me is none of my business. That is such a tremendous weight off my shoulders.

What I want you to understand is feeling whole, complete, enough, special, precious, nurtured, heard, beautiful, valuable, loved will cause us to soar and activate our full potential. Although you will be faced with challenges that will test your integrity, this journey is all about how you respond to those challenges. Choose to grow through the challenges and never accept being victim. We must become habitual at immersing ourselves in all that it takes to maintain our wholeness. Once we master this, we will be unstoppable, and most of all feel fulfilled, grounded and full of joy in our hearts. We then pass this positive energy and perspective on to our children which will create a pure, blissful environment. This also will set the foundation and tone as to how they develop relationships in their future as they grow through life.

Did you know that more than 80% of women don't feel whole? Why is there only a small percentage of us stepping into our wholeness? Many of us experience feelings of being trapped, feeling stuck, unlovable, stressed and not good enough. The reasoning behind this astonishing statistic is that we live cyclically. We repeat patterns. We're not just recycling our own baggage, but that of our mothers and probably multiple generations who came before us. We inherit their struggles, their beliefs and values in many cases, even the outdated and non-serving ones that may have been useful long ago but not in today's world.

Awareness of the negative patterns and cyclical behavior we exhibit means we must do something about it. Here are **3 Actionable Steps** you can take to help break the negative cycles in your life right now:

1. Look at yourself in the mirror. Not just on the surface but I challenge you to look into the soul through the pupils of that little girl who was once 5 years old who didn't die. Look deeply to connect to her little heart within.

2. Once connected treat her as you desire to be treated. Only speak to or about yourself as you would speak to an innocent child whom you loved as your own child and whom you wanted to grow up without any insecurities. She is oh so precious. She deserves the LOVE and treatment that she always desired. Only YOU can allow her that simple desire.

YOU ARE THE GATEKEEPER to her HAPPINESS and no one else!

3. Change your environment to one which supports the needs of this valuable precious human being. Say "NO" when you would too easily please others above yourself. Say "YES" to your own needs by putting yourself first. Put the oxygen mask on yourself first and then reach out to help others. It's not selfish. Remember, it's not only about YOU, but it's also how you treat yourself which affects those around you.

Notes

Notes

"Raising Emotionally Healthy Children"

I AM an overcomer. Even though my ex-husband is no longer a part of my life, my children and I are going to be just fine! I have survived the most difficult time in my life and through that process, I found true value in investing in my personal development. Although it took having a few breakdowns, I view this experience as time needed to heal as well as to get healthy mentally and emotionally in order for my children to be taken care of in a loving, healthy environment. With the challenges that motherhood brings, I embrace them because nothing is more rewarding than coming home after a hard day at work and seeing the smiles on your children's face because they are happy to see you. Nothing is more rewarding than to be able to pour into your children positive, forward thinking principles and morals that build confidence in who they are becoming. I am committed to building a strong foundation which helps them create healthy habits and a healthy mindset.

I have taught them core biblical principles that help them practice healthy coping skills as well as hold me accountable to stick to coping in a healthy manner. I also instill in them respect not only for others but for themselves.

Divorce not only rocks your world but it also rocks your children's world. Children of every age need both of their parents. Children naturally want their parents to be together and may ask what happened and why mommy and daddy are not together. I help my children understand why mommy and daddy didn't work out and are not together. I encourage and teach them that it is ok to love both of us and that it is not their fault that we are not together.

Three years after the divorce was final and not being present in the children's life, my ex-husband decided to come around. Our son was 5, and our daughter was 7. It was really challenging, but we have been working it out. I never wanted to rob my children of the opportunity to build a relationship with their dad, despite what we went through. I always tell them that despite what happened, their dad will always be their Hero and mommy will always be their Shero!

There are times that the children may see or feel some energy that doesn't feel so good between mom and dad. That's when both parties re-adjust and become mature enough to let it go and agree to be amicable for the sake of the children. Should there be a time where one parent does not want to be amicable in a certain situation, we step away from the situation, come back at another time and agree to a solution at the right moment.

Research shows nothing is more traumatic in life than a divorce other than death. It affects both the adults and children involved.

As I was conducting research for this book, I discovered that divorce is the second of the top five stressful life situations, death of a loved one being first.

Even if we are glad to get rid of our ex-spouse, divorce is a major stressor in our lives. In addition to causing us to feel stress, it can also stress out our children. Many couples are so wrapped up with their own emotions during a divorce that they fail to notice the impact of the situation on their children. Chances are that the kids are feeling quite a bit of turmoil, even if they are too young to understand what is really going on. In fact, younger children can experience even more stress than older children in the case of their parent's divorce because they cannot put their emotions into words, nor can they understand that daddy or mommy going away has nothing to do with them. To a young child, everything in the world has something to do with them.

Many commentators have said for years that divorce is worse than death because many times with death there is closure but with divorce, closure, especially when kids are involved can be hard to find.

Here are a few things that have helped me raise emotionally healthy children:

- **Always continue to grow as an adult because your growth helps them grow.**
  Set the example and take the initiative in continued personal development. Show them by grabbing a book and reading. Take them to some of your personal development seminars. Put them around the positive company you keep. Have a mentor and get them a mentor as well.

- **Keep the lines of communication open for your children**
  Let them know they can talk to you and show them through your actions that you will not judge them. Make sure that you impress upon them the importance of venting and expressing themselves. Create a support system of family and friends that you trust, and they feel comfortable with and have them be a sounding board outside of you if they would like to vent to someone else other than you. Allow them to feel the different feelings that come with divorce and let them know it is normal to have those feelings.

- **Avoid negative talk about dad**
  Don't talk down about dad to them or to others in their presence. This behavior creates resentment in children very early. This resentment can be towards you and/or the other parent. More than likely toward the parent that is projecting the negative talk.

At the time of publishing this book, my three children are now 16, 10 and 8. They were fairly young when the divorce occurred, however, my oldest remembers a lot. I create time for the two of us so that she can vent and express herself. She is my daughter from another relationship and now understands what has taken place. She is very close to her father. Although teenagers will be teenagers, I am proud to say that she is in the AP program at school and very sharp. My younger two from the marriage are now building a strong relationship with their father and as time goes on we get stronger as a family. My ex-husband and I are making strides to successfully co-parent. It is a work in progress and we take things day by day.

Notes

Notes

CHAPTER 9

"The Sacrifice"

The vicious cycle of trading my time for money and working on someone else's vision while someone else raised my children was grueling to me. The times where my children would get sick and knowing I had to call off of work and lose pay to care for my children was very stressful. I had little to no support when it came to that. My desire was to be able to work for myself with time and financial freedom so that I can be available to my children as they needed me on my time and no one else's. I worked hard on creating different opportunities to create time and freedom. I failed forward a lot of times. In the midst of creating new opportunities, I made the best of the time I did have to spend quality time with the children. This was also the reason why I did not date for so many years after my divorce because I wanted to give my children the extra time I had outside of work. Time is the biggest sacrifice for single mothers.

I find that we also tend to sacrifice and put our dreams and lives on hold to fulfill our children's dreams and goals. I personally feel that we should create balance in the midst of the chaos of what being a single mother comes with. When my oldest daughter was three, my aunt invited me to go on a Caribbean Cruise. I battled in my own head the possibility of me being away from her for so long, so far away. I thought her dad would make it difficult for me to go. I also battled with being confident that if I were to go, would he be effective at taking care of her with me gone so far away and for a whole eight days. I had a conversation with my mother, and she emphasized that he was her father and my daughter would be okay. My mother impressed upon me that if I was confident in my delivery in trusting that I was ok with him to care for our daughter, he would be more apt to be ok to keep her while I was away. I stepped out on faith, had the discussion and got his blessing on allowing me to go.

Ever since my emotional breakdown, I now speak up to my family and communicate what I need. I have traveled more and been out of the country a few more times with the support of my village.

It is ok to plan a get away from the children with the right support system and effectively communicating with the other parent. I am looking forward to planning a few get away trips with the children so that they can experience and enjoy the other side of life as well.

Half of the battles that we create with the other parent is in our heads or perhaps in theirs. Please don't make assumptions and don't take ANYTHING personal.

Know who your trusting support system is. If you don't have one, look for individuals who would be willing to support you. Ask questions. Ask for help. It's okay to be vulnerable and transparent. Do not isolate yourself or pretend to have it all together.

ASK and you shall receive. SEEK and you will find. KNOCK and the door will opened.

It's vital to your mental and emotional state to take time for yourself to re-center. Then after taking time to yourself, treat the children. Children are resilient and will understand once you develop effective communication with them.

I encourage you to:

- *Get that massage*
- *Take that trip*
- *Start that business*
- *Get your nails done*
- *Go out to dinner*
- *Go dancing*
- *Have your "Zen" moments*

Get some adult time in, IT IS OK!

Notes

Notes

CHAPTER 10

<u>"Dating and Falling in Love Again as a Mom"</u>

Right after my divorce, I thought that I would never get married again. I abhorred men. With the history of my biological father and really wanting a stable relationship with him, to growing up with an abusive stepfather, to my ex-husband, I just thought I was doomed. I started to think it's not in my cards to be in a happy, thriving, loving relationship with a man, the right man. I realized I had a misguided belief of happiness. I wasn't genuinely happy with Ayesha. I depended on my marriage to be happy. I depended on my husband to make me happy. I wasn't truly whole and neither was he which is why we attracted each other.

I continued to focus on my personal growth and learned about mentorship, I created a more positive view towards men and dating again. Two years after my divorce I decided that I would no longer be closed to the idea of dating. I spent five years just working on my inner me, no committed relationships. I had to take into consideration of how my children would be affected once I did decide to date.

I set a goal for myself that when my youngest child turned five years old, I would start dating again.

<u>Here are a few things I took into consideration BEFORE I started dating:</u>

• Lay the Groundwork for Dating

I spoke to my children about how they felt if mommy started seeing a man who is not their dad. The timing of having this conversation had to be right. My children are of age to understand what is going on. I paid attention to how they responded. Fortunately, my children were good with it because they desire a full family environment just as I do. However, I learned that if the children resisted the idea, not to adjust my decision to date. I was fully aware that the journey may be a little rocky but I was prepared to keep the lines of communication open.

• Pace Yourself while Dating

Don't rush the dating process. When you do decide to date be slow about introducing the children to the new guy too quickly because you are getting to know him. Do not spend all your free time with the new person you are dating and put your children on the back burner. This opens your children up to resentment. The family unit must remain your priority, and the children should never be viewed as an obstacle to your new relationship.

• Expect some Ups and Downs

Keep in mind the children's loyalty to the other parent. They will often become confused and conflicted if they truly like your new partner. On the other hand, they may witness the pain of the other parent if they are upset about your decision to pursue a relationship with the new person. Allow them time to sort out their feelings. Be discerning and objectively measure your new partner's attitude and connection towards your children. There will always be room for adjustment but just make sure to always treat your children with respect.

I had to also realize that there was more to consider when dating with children. So as I began to start my journey to date, I was very careful about environment and energy. I was not just casually dating I was dating with the view to get married. I began to surround myself around positive, loving couples and ironically a few of my mentors were successfully married couples.

I began to attract all kinds of men, and not all were the type I was looking to have in my life. As I began to evolve, more qualified bachelors started to show up which allowed me to have healthy options, which will lead to the right one finding me.

I had to be more specific about what I wanted in the man I would date and possibly marry. I knew I wanted a man who not only loved God, but was God-fearing. I desired a mate who was a loving, responsible father. I knew I wanted a man who was stable mentally and emotionally as well as financially. Communication, respect loyalty and integrity are all key factors. He has to have and take responsibility on his own, NO MAMA'S BOYS! It is important to set standards and ask specifically for what you want. Do I expect perfection, NO. We all are flawed, but it is important that you know what you want and what you will be willing to work through with the other person.

I am now happily dating again. I am meeting more qualified men that have the similar core values as I do. I am grateful. I am now operating in wholeness, and I am much more in tune with my inner me.

Notes

CHAPTER 11

"A Vulnerable Moment with Other Single Moms"

"Making sacrifices as a single Mom naturally I put my daughter first forgetting about myself. Forgetting to nurture and take care of me so I can be my best self for her. Being a single mom has given me strength and taught me how to persevere through anything life throws me. Being a single mom I have had to put my personal needs and dreams aside, to make my daughter my number one priority. I've given up so much for my daughter so she can have the life she deserves, and sometimes I feel like it's just not enough. Making sacrifices as a single mom has not been easy but yet rewarding." ~ **Lashea Singleton**

"Single motherhood has always been about loving my kids through loving myself first. Most would interpret that as being selfish, however for me that is my love language. I always felt like this was the best way to be a single mom. I don't understand how I can give my children the world if I had never understood what that looked like. In my opinion, the best way to love on your children is by emulating what that looks like." **~Tasha Sims**

"I'm a thirty-five-year-old single mother of two very smart and talented teenagers. I got married at 19 and had my children back to back when I was 21 and 22. By the age of 26, I was divorced and had to face my biggest fear of raising two children alone. To add to the stress, I was unemployed, and my mortgage became due. I felt like a failure. I found a journal I used to write in when I was in high school, and I decided to set out to accomplish those goals. I gained employment and returned to school. By age 29 I had earned my BS in Business Management from Fashion Institute of Design Merchandise, and I was so proud to hear my children cheering for me as I walked the stage. Today I am a professional in the fashion industry, I make six figures, and I travel throughout the year both with and without my children. I would say every dream in my journal has come true and I continue to set new goals for myself. Being a single mother is such a joy to me, I see it as the fuel to the fire that burns deep in the depth of my desire to show my children they can overcome any challenge and achieve anything." ~ **Denshai Lee**

"Being a single mother, I had to first realize that I didn't have anyone to fall back on, although I did have family. Sometimes, the judgments would come out. The 'You are always at work,' 'Your kids need you,' started to get to me. I started to feel even worse. With long hours of missing homework, bath and bedtime stories, six days a week, having that one day off I wanted to just rest. However, with kids, I had to sacrifice that rest because all they want is you. It started to make me frustrated that I didn't have an outlet. I suffered from depression from just not being pleased with how my life was going. Missing the quality time with them and all my kid's activities, barely making ends meet, I began growing weary of this vicious cycle. I just knew it had to be a different way. After surrounding myself with some positive people, I started changing my perspective. They were very encouraging. Personal development was and still is one of the methods I utilize and apply to myself every day."
~**Mercedes Richardson**

"I've been in this incredible space of what the world refers to as a single mom for 15 years now. I must say that it has been the most challenging, uplifting, deflating, loving space to ever experience. There has been plenty of back-breaking challenges that I would never have seen coming, including the death of my daughter's father in 2012. Needless to say, that was the last straw that REALLY broke the camel's back. As you can possibly imagine, my life was totally slammed up against the wall. As a wardrobe stylist, I experienced recurring job loss, and so many monthly eviction notices that I could teach a course. My self-confidence was depleted and of course, remembering to somehow remain a 'strong mother' for my emotionally drained daughter was almost unreachable. Fast forward to the present moment; I am finding my way again, but this time with an unshakeable and loving village of Sistar friends and men of great fortitude. I have created a selfless movement called M.O.M. or Matriarchs of Magnificence for myself and all the other fabulous M.O.M.'s in the world who choose to lead a path of pure, incredible amazement, and make a resounding difference in our own separate spaces."
~**Missie Shealey**

"When I walked out of a 10-year marriage, I didn't think about the fact that I would be walking into the world of single motherhood. Trying to juggle a career and parenting, I was quickly hit with fear, guilt, and depression. I shed many tears. The first year took a toll on me physically, emotionally, and financially.

Between the constant harassment from my ex-husband, divorce court, and the cries of my kids for their dad, I wanted to give up so many times. I was scared, but it was the love I had for my children that strengthened me each day.

Eventually, with the help of GOD, my family, and friends, I decided not to allow my situation to define me. I started reading the Bible faithfully every night by myself and with my kids. My heart slowly started to heal, and—importantly—I started to forgive myself. All this helped me find the motivation and drive for life again, and I started getting more involved in my kids' lives, getting them into sports, music, dance, and more. They deserved the best of me, and I was determined to give it to them." ~**Kongite Tesfaye**

"I am a single mother of 4 who fled an abusive relationship from Oklahoma City to Dallas, Texas in 2011. Working as a nurse at one of the top hospitals in Dallas, I ended up homeless and sleeping in my SUV with my kids. I was blessed to be able to find relief in a transitional shelter. After graduating from the program and finding a place to live, we maintained by being self-sufficient for years. I volunteered as a life coach at the shelter until I was able to get the chance to be hired full-time. I worked for several years and published my first book, "Love Letters" in 2017. We have been hungry, devastated and near death, but we survived. I had no choice but to respect and endure the process. It was painful, but my kids and I would not have learned how to lean and depend on God without this life happening. I had to be taught even as a parent and adult about my finances and budgeting in the transitional program. I am now a published author, speaker, licensed minister, and life coach. Soon to be grandmother and raising my amazing children who are excelling in academics and extracurricular sports. Without the pain of my process, I would have never birthed my purpose." ~ **Eunice Jones**

"Embracing the life of a single mom has been both rewarding and challenging. The challenges I face makes me more humble, stronger and resilient. There are times when I get extremely stressed about not having emotional and financial support from my kids' dad. During these times, I sometimes struggle with unforgiveness toward their dad for not being present. I then have to remind myself that unforgiveness will kill you. I realize that forgiveness doesn't mean that you forgot, it means that you just don't dwell on it anymore and that I cannot go forward by looking back. I have to consciously reset my mood and remind myself to continue to trust God and that he has not and will not leave me or forsake me. Through meditating on God's word and seeking him in all things, I find the strength to push through and know that it will be ok. I've been a single mom now for 13 years and am just now starting to make time for myself, even if it's to sit quietly alone and listen to the birds' chirp. I've grown to not care about the little things and I to appreciate each day that I am given the opportunity to even be a mom. At the end of the day I count it all a joy." ~ **Sonia Conner**

"I never thought that I would be a single mother. Not that anyone does, but I honestly never envisioned it as a part of my life story. My biggest fear was falling into the negative stereotype of being just another young, single black mother. I was determined to create the absolute best life possible for myself and my twin daughters. They were the biggest driving force behind starting my business, and I love being able to include them in my journey of pursuing my dreams. I wanted to be their first and biggest role model. The road hasn't always been smooth. I've faced many obstacles: job loss, a devastating car accident that left me unable to walk for nearly a year, hitting rock bottom financially, and a battle with depression. However, through prayer and a strong support team I was able to overcome it all and prove that a setback is just a setup for a comeback, and no matter what you go through in life, you can bounce back and succeed." ~ **Nikola Ahaiwe**

I handpicked these single mothers and I am so grateful that they agreed to share a little of their "challenge-to-success" journey with us. This is to show you that there are plenty of single mothers out there turning their breakdowns into breakthroughs.

I chose 9 mothers because the number 9 has a powerful meaning. The number 9 symbolizes a few things but what stood out to me is that it symbolizes patience, harmony, inspiration, the perfection of ideas and one who accomplished divine will. With that being said, we as mothers have to be patient with our children; we have to work within HIS divine will to inspire them. We are responsible for their well-being because they are gifts to us no matter how they were conceived. They are God's perfect creation.

Notes

CHAPTER 12

"Giving Back"

Service to many leads to greatness. I find that when you give help to someone in need, you facilitate strong encouragement. Showing compassion and giving kindness can truly be uplifting. It serves as a sense of faith and acts as a tremendous source of renewal for someone who is truly hurting. Helping people for me sets an example for my children.

Someone reached out and helped me, and it changed my life. I always wanted to create a way to help others. I find that it sets a positive and powerful tone for the day. In my research, I found that giving to others induces a high level of fulfillment and happiness that radiates an attractiveness that others are drawn to.

I have been in a space where I didn't give back because I created the belief in my mind that if I could barely make it in life myself, why help the next person tying this belief in with thinking that it was just about giving back monetarily, and that hindered me from a lot of abundance on so many levels. I learned that giving doesn't always have to be monetary. I learned this a few years ago when a dear friend of mine shared with me her philosophy about giving. What stood out the most to me is when she said, "You're not truly living until you're freely giving," This friend was Tiffany A. Rose, Founder of one of the largest non-profit organizations that feed and clothe families in need in Los Angeles, California. *My Friends House LA.* is one of the largest homeless communities worldwide. From then on, I started finding ways I could give to others. My children and I would do our spring cleaning and donate our clothes that we couldn't wear anymore. Not only does this help us feel happy and fulfilled when giving to others but it is a joy to see the majority of those we are being a blessing to feel happy, too

I grew weary of seeing and feeling the pain so much so that I have and am still creating the new cycle for my children so they can be happier. After restructuring your life, continue to grow and be the best human being you can be. Grab the hand of another Mom and help her grow.

Before you help another person, the first hand you grab should be that of your child (ren). We are so quick to grab a stranger's hand to help them first, but the growth starts at home. I was guilty of being quick to help a stranger and failed to pay attention to my child's emotional needs first. It wasn't intentional but because I needed the pain to stop, I wanted my situation to get better. I thought helping others was the right way to be an example to my children by giving back. The truth is, if you are grabbing a stranger's hand first before helping your child, you are displaying a false sense of empowerment. There is nothing wrong with giving back but it is imperative that we keep things in perspective. Take of yourself first, cultivate your relationship with your Higher Power, then pour into your kids and everyone else should experience the overflow of your blessings.

I am currently working on a foundation created to help underprivileged single moms thrive and find their happy. I am convinced that the challenges that were placed before me, as I've shared in this book, were not for me but to help me become stronger to be able to help the next mother in need going through hardship. I have a deep passion to use my story to empower other women. If I can do it, they can do it. Stay tuned as I am currently in formation with the details of this incredible non-profit organization guaranteed to positively impact single-parent families, one mom at a time.

Notes

Notes

Conclusion

The principles, tips, and ideas I've presented in this book are to help you reconnect with your kids and to help you all move on with your lives as successfully as possible after a divorce. We all have different goals and different objectives, but if your goal is to be emotionally healthy as a parent with emotionally healthy kids who love and respect you and have healed and gained enough self-awareness to have healthy and meaningful relationships, we've achieved our goal.

I really believe the root of the issue with everything in life is spiritual. We are all spiritual beings on this planet, and we cannot truly love and be loved until we forgive ourselves and others.

Whether you decide to raise your children as a single parent or get involved in another relationship, make sure you remain whole. Safeguard yourself by staying around environments and people who generate positive energy.

As I've stated in the beginning, I'm not here to highlight the negative statistics of divorce and single motherhood. However, my assignment is to empower you with the positive side of single motherhood. Statistics show that children raised by a single mother has multiple negative effects, however, here are **10 remarkable benefits of being raised by a single mother:**

1. Strength: The strength to do it alone if necessary. A role model who never left and who never gave up.

2. Courage: The absolute courage to do a job meant for two people alone and often with uncertainties.

3. Loyalty: The devotion as a single mother to her children despite the hardship and difficulty and less than ideal circumstances.

4. Reliability: The reliability and steadfast parenting that it takes to let a child know they can count on you no matter the circumstances.

5. Independence: The independence to do whatever is needed despite the fear of being raised by just one parent.

6. Selflessness: the degree of selflessness to take on the responsibility of two parents without resentment or complaint.

7. Intimacy: the level of closeness and emotional intimacy that is essential for children to feel safe in every area of their lives.

8. Resourceful: The resourcefulness it takes to problem solve everything often without the time, money or support that is needed.

9. Resilience: The determination to provide and be there. Being the example that giving up is not an option.

10. Gratefulness: The extreme effortless love which represents the remarkable gratitude for being a mom regardless of the fact that it might be done alone. This may be the greatest benefit because it conveys indescribable and unconditional love despite the unconventional circumstances.

Being a single mother should not be considered a burden but it is a tremendous blessings. Keep this guide handy when you experience moments of sadness or overwhelm. You are a survivor and YOU ARE MORE THAN ENOUGH!

ABOUT THE AUTHOR

Ayesha R. Goodall, a Los Angeles native, is a Supermom of 3 amazing children. With an extensive background in Real Estate and Psychology, she learned that going through the vicious cycle of trading her time for money in corporate America kept her struggling financially. She realized that she could not tap into her creative gifts and become the best version of herself living someone else's dream.

Ayesha stepped out on faith, as a single mother, using her natural entrepreneurial talents and resourcefulness to venture out in finding her niche behind helping others. Over time, she discovered her purpose and passion and became a true visionary in creating her path to success. She has mastered turning her BREAKDOWNS into BREAKTHROUGHS. Her ability to take the initiative to help herself first and in turn help her children has allowed her to create a platform for her clients to experience what it feels like to believe bigger, think better, speak better, look better and feel better. She is a mindset and wellness coach, speaker, author, philanthropist and women's empowerment advocate.

EMPOWER.ENLIGHTEN.ELEVATE

Book Ayesha to Speak

Ayesha is an incredible speaker, CEO of GoodZen Consulting Services. Ayesha's message of empowerment and passion to help women around the world turn their breakdowns into breakthroughs is a message that will benefit your women's group, corporate event, networking group, conferences and more.

If you are ready for your audience to soar and add a dynamic WOW factor with takeaways that your audience can utilize right away, please contact her for your next event.
You can book her by sending an email to
ayesha@goodzenconsulting.com